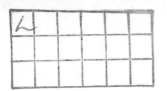

Barbecue of the Primitives

Philip Salom was born in Perth in 1950, and currently teaches creative writing at Curtin University, where he has also been a Writer-in-Residence. He takes an active interest in live performance, having read in the U.K., Singapore and at the Struga International Poetry Festival in Yugoslavia, and also established Disk Readings, a Perth performance venue. Salom's three previous books (*The Silent Piano, The Projectionist* and *Sky Poems*) have won many awards, and he is the only poet ever to have won the Commonwealth Poetry Prize twice – in 1981 and 1987.

Barbecue of the Primitives

PHILIP SALOM

University of Queensland Press

First published 1989 by University of Queensland Press,
Box 42, St Lucia, Queensland, Australia

Typeset by University of Queensland Press
Printed in Australia by Australian Print Group, Maryborough

Distributed in the USA and Canada by
International Specialized Book Services, Inc.,
5602 N.E. Hassalo Street, Portland, Oregon 97213-3640

Creative writing program assisted by
the Literature Board of the Australia
Council, the Federal Government's arts
funding and advisory body

Arts for
Australians
Australia Council

Cataloguing in Publication Data
National Library of Australia

ISBN 0 7022 2221 6

Salom, Philip, 1950– .
   Barbecue of the primitives.

   I. Title. (Series : UQP poetry).

A821'.3

for Tom Shapcott

Contents

Acknowledgments

Poems from this collection have appeared in the *Canberra Times*, *Westerly*, *Island Magazine*, *Southern Review*, *Prairie Schooner*, *Kunapipi*, *Portrait* (Fremantle Arts Centre Press), *Margins* (FACP), and the *Mattara* anthologies – "Poem of Thanksgiving and other poems", "Properties of the Poet" and "The International Terminal".

I would like to thank the Literature Board for its encouragement and support and for a Category A Writer's Fellowship in 1987 when many of these poems were worked on.

Lament on Deaths in Infancy

for my mother

The wind should die for a second
the house go mute. On it goes, as night
shuffles and tutt-tutts, meaning nothing.
The roof leans heavily as a drunk,
its iron crackling like ganglia.
The wind oscillates and observes
all things are animate.

The heat moved heavily, did not observe
all things were animate, but
one weight alive, and one weight
where death had placed its heavy, eye-closed copy,
its blue baby.

He had little chance, six months
of air, two worlds of blood.
It was not the labels on the bottles
they got wrong, but the labels
on the bodies: my father's blood test.
He passed, but the staff or test had failed
and your son, my brother,
failed it for six months straight,
after trying, still the angel in him,
to pump it right, to play its awful music
when all the time it was killing him.

Entering summer, he had done too much.
Everything external so neat and tragic
Rhesus negative. He would die in perfect health.
Entering summer, you were impossible grief.
The summer was your grief.

Two eyes will find the breast and see
this world milkily and brief, alive
for a day or a week or months in what begins but ends
like a mild waking and turning over in sleep.
The universal gaze has been returned.

Where among the worlds
does this gasp and stare become reality?
The world is measured here that hung
from the umbilicus like easy fruit
and the world but not the same world
the fearful and painful world
is weighed all the greater, through grief.

What is kept alive
is the whole manner of behaviour;
the crease in school shorts,
seeing the light sit well upon three sons,
engaging rituals: school bags and bikes;
the world pushes down upon their pedals
and as the future turns
they disappear into the mist.

There is no place the grieving go
to grieve and to escape grief.
Going because there is no choice
but to go where there is no trace.
Where does the power of grief go?

At the cemetery, one metre of soil
goes down forever.
The universe does not exhaust itself.
It takes. And takes
after the wrenching out, the sluice
and the giving. It

lays down the world, pains and passions
laid down like teeth before the gums.
So the lands have place and the maps
say this or that is the place . . .

I've heard men tutt and click
as tongue and palate pat a woman
sadly on the head, meaning
Poor thing . . . but really . . . she should be over it by now.
And this is sounded not for her but for
the world to hear his desperation.

Where does a father wail who never gave
the sphere unto the spheres?
Never having been so full −
how to comprehend so empty?

Pregnancy is life's chain letter
but nothing delivered is returned.
Death is life's long postscript
but the letter is too heavy.
You must pay extra, again and again.
You have the reddest eyes to read.
The universal words have been returned.

If you are too knowing to rail against death
this you despair of and rail against
that same knowingness.
Behind emotion there is emotion
and it is death. Not grief, but death.
It gives pain its place
if not the map entirely.
It has no tense
but the perfect, now and always.

This ironic summer, you read in papers, not knowing
we read it too, in Florence, in Dante's city:
Inferno in London underground, 20 dead. How, safe,

could we guess at your endless circle: fearing us,
seeing him, among the dead, 34 years that passed
plunge burning on the platform underground,
buffeting along the rails, at each point
unable to step out when the carriage doors
slide back, and the world peoples off into
its anxious colours. Half of them, quite black.

As the nanny who held me in your place was black
while the angel fought and I imagined, even wanted,
I could be cause of it. Who wanted love
in white and black, who climbed uphill in summer
when no-one could see enough, or see right.

So when my son was born, there were times
objects would scare me in my hands.
I had to carry love, carry past the black
of angels, carry love despite irrationality
of images cutting in the darkness.

This is for you. In the beginning
and always, the depth all parents carry
deepest where death will always be, upon the living.
The cure is long, and outlasts summers.
It is your life, the perfect tense. It lasts forever.

The Wind Has Panels

Not the seminar kind. The wind has panels
like an endless series of opening doors
but far more subtle than doors: I think
of panels in Thailand, where the walls of houses

fold out and air moves like a calming sexual act,
like ecstasy, like walking inside the wind
when panel after panel admits you. Forget
the days when they don't, when knocking there

buffets and resists you. On the common days
like these, fights break out on the corner, someone
is shot. A Jumbo crashes after take-off
looking, in devastation, like it hit the sky head on

and mountainous. Was refused admittance.
Such is the grief in families of the victims.
Their faces crease and flatten, worn back
by wind, pushed flat by the panels in the wind.

The wind has dreams. It dreams its panels
altogether cease, like Buddha's final meditation,
like Christ's emphatic vision of the will of God.
Yet the wind awakens. The wind has panels.

After the Building

for Greg Stratton

You caught me from the start,
saying you built three dark rooms.
In the sensual world of wood and sweat
precision rules, both saw and chisel
are dangerous; wood does not recover
from its wounds − unless the cuts
exactly fit − or wounds become a world.
But all this to keep the light *out*.
Made me understand how I had seen
building as illumination, ours or anyone's.

That much. Once, too, you told me
poems I wrote addressed to "you", the second person,
caught *you*, the you who cut these rooms
to wander and walk and turn the cutting edge
planing the reference off across your selves.
But I meant the double-ended arrow,
writing as illumination, mine or anyone's.

These rooms have eyes: remote, in boxes,
changing, compounded like an insect's,
seeing through the laws of energy and time.
This is what you built. After sleep,
three rooms glowing redly, softer than lips;
and always, shuttling from light to dark
illumination stilled among the flow.

I see you, invited back: those dark rooms
feeding under reddish glow, seeing images
of the camera's double-arrow, cutting there
among the trays, among old chemicals
of the universe — of what no longer is
but now appears when you, you, you,
three rooms, three illuminations
sit squarely, balanced, and still.

Something seems alive in there, something fey.
But is it sensuous as lips, or is it more
like soul? Going back again, finding pause
between its incarnations? You made the rooms
that now are someone else's; taken
your tools and gone back home.
Something else is watching there, quite new.

There is Nothing Like a Room

There is nothing like the single room
to carry more, like a swank hotel, ensuite
to paradise, or floored onto the melancholy streets,
balconied above the ocean and its breeze,
from windows teasing out to mists and chilly paddocks.
Or rooms we carry with us, rooms like nagging parents.

A larger room, eight years ago, bed and robes
veneered in walnut, the mirrors oval and immaculate,
ourselves making love, skin-long in the centre:
no room is quite so sensuous again.
Being then unlimited, time was sensuous, and light,
loving us through intervals, loving us alone,
indulgently, light, third of our menage à trois, whispering
take your time, take all of me, in light
or half-light, *love me, take* . . .

This room folds into the room I work in
just as flesh folds into flesh, infolding
though the labour ward, the centrepiece
ourselves, shaken by the image of an easy birth
we were not to see, brought into the labour
by mistake. Until flesh, the all-you of flesh
after 24 hours, was two. The wild electric-
pain had earthed you. I cannot guess
which parts had been its terminals.

The room empties of the air from then.
I hear your voices – now the breeze has come –
as if upon a balcony, or like posters
flapping on the wall beside me, then still again.
Layer on layer, like glazes and additions

on our first and brilliant images, more than
sunlight's subtle laminations on our skin.
The day is cooling from an afternoon so warm.
Last night I dreamt I was a child again.

The Hostel: Remembering a Dream

Austere building on the hill, weatherboard and stilts
where the ocean breathes and power-lines gleam like
    filaments.

No sound in the dream, no wind. But there's no forgetting
    them.
I wander the empty dormitories. Sunlight

lingers on the sills, the lit afternoon side
that holds hard in my images now the rooms are filled:

like a wall of portraits, adults stand at each window
in violent chiaroscuro, each face half-lost in glare,

each face raw with light, as if it burns their features out
like over-exposed photographs. Their adolescent faces come
    back

in camera — each f stop shows as much again dementia:
two of them kick a naked youngster on the shower floor,

a gauntlet of wet towels for another — each swung tip
startling, stripping skin, until the welts read like cuneiform

or the symbols of a violent choreography.
A boy is hung from a high window at midnight

by one foot. His body is a garish star
tapping the universe of its imagery.

It is reactionary as it is ancient, more than
the eight generations of levelling that led here.

In the moonlight his aggressors gleam, light gone
solid as metal on their bodies. They are timeless, robots;

his body is a pendulum at this slow face
filled with passion. And if their bodies range like numbers

it's because they are universal constants. Living is a popular
    art
but must be woken, slapped into its radical conformity.

The neutral eye's deposed by violence and sex
like any revolution. A boy is forced into bed

with another, or once with an octopus three days dead.
Armlocks reveal every sexual detail of a charmer and his
    girlfriends

until the hearers come out in goose-flesh and with their
    fingers
prod his girl-flesh, learning this language like communal
    braille.

And from the ocean blows a psychic wind: of impulses
that later will return, laden with images.

Even silence will have an image: the sun-lit passage
and slowly percolating dust, or the night of crystal sets

each dormitory a long glass diode in conductive darkness.
Through headphones to boys lying still as capacitors

civilisation glows like a juke box into local song,
waves of the outer language, phrases from the western ocean

flash through wire aerials looped around the room,
thin convolutions of the brain.

At last they will seem so civilised — who knows
how thorough their severing has been? For now the force is
    resolute.

And now the adults turn from the windows
and the dreamer waits. The first severing was momentous.

City at Dusk

The sun sinks into the summer haze
as if the west was endless veils of skin,
to be shed at the flash-point of brilliance
by the tireless dancer at the End of the Apocalypse,
a Salome of sorts, but Shiva more probably,
fluent and indifferent, four-armed
to wrap us twice over, to play both sides
in the circle of perfect circles.

I feel it all without the music.
This tone-deaf dancer, out there, waiting,
a metal character that has no powers of irony
to know his favourite places will destroy him.
He may descend into this land like an avatar
but incendiary, measured in gigatonnes.
He drinks the poisoned sea, ponders destruction.

If ocean has old power, here is earth-power,
the old land-power of Aboriginals.
But I sit on top of white-power: drinking as
everywhere on soaring platforms the office lights
come on; intensifying voices in the purple time,
first the basses, then the tenors,
then the pin-like legato of the women.

I see the highways
like sinews of light entering the bulking darkness.
Cars twist in rows up carriageways, their tail-lights
red as flame, each car dancing on its oval
blade of light. They glide over bridges like microdots,
onto flyovers like endless flows of isotopes.

It is city, on all sides, the thinking ocean,
the dance of intellect. It is unthinkable
to think of London, Dresden, shorelines

that broke like standing shells (their eerie atonal music).
Here is nuclear shoreline, the music would be flat.
We are part of another ceremony, of tea: tableland and places
    set;
the cups are in space, drifting; the saucers
tilt along the coast to catch the bitter drops.

Every time has borne its wrong. I tilt my glass,
light curves and floats upon the spirit —
to sip is to feed the world into itself.
To sip and read so many schoolkids think they'll die
among the dancing atoms.

It is dusk. The universal time, and time perhaps
to leave experiments of melancholy.
The power of simply living dances in us all.
Shiva's foot rests on Apmassara,
demon of forgetfulness . . .

But somehow at dusk
the city is a glowing hangar:
there is preparedness among the massive lifts,
the cranes waiting like constant steel insects
intent on flight. It is the space-deck, worriedly
laid before us, where the craft seem waiting
in our minds, waiting as they always have,
glittering upon their oil.

Ghazal on Signs of Love and Occupation

For Helena

Someone's licked a finger, touched it to the mirror.
A bleary, innocent fingerprint, but yes, it's me.

Remember gaudiness passing for emotion on TV – yet
spray-can love, in tunnels, questions our art-forms with
flourish.

Imagine at night, the torch hiccupping, the youth bent.
She fucks him so he thinks it's love. But he makes his print.

See the young and rich pressed on their sweet enamel –
BMW,
more talk of art seems less and less. Give me the tunnel.

I see aristocratic citizens in the street, columns of faces saying
we don't want your challenges. Out of this make literature.

Racket rises from the block next door – bulldozers
pirouette in the dust, a place in the universe is laid bare.

Bricks all say the same thing. An ambulance makes
donkey-tones
in traffic. Water-pipes bang from visitation, not you in the
shower.

When first you struck the keyboard, you found its twin
waiting in your head. Our love goes on. My pen is poised in
air.

Inquiry of the Spirit Body

What shape does it have? Is it opaque and worn inside?
Is it homunculus, pea-shaped and chuckling in the pineal?
A transparent sleeve my body wears like perspiration
or clammy from excitation or from fear?
Stroke my arm and shoulder, then sweep my front's
cascade of skin — surely you feel nothing
extra? Is it seen by changes, by gradations,
like a lover's body browning slowly through summer,
or paling, suddenly, from standing near fluorescence?
Perhaps it sits, an energetic cloud (esoteric I'm afraid)
a held flare, magnesium dancing to the inner eye,
the third . . . Perhaps it floats, stands, sits or slumps down
on the table beside me, my hand pushing through it
as I write. Or does it keep an easy distance like a dog?

Perhaps it is myself on the leash, silver
and a mongrel but for my sixth-sense search,
this dogged sniffing at all corners.
Does it carry scars for wounds not yet received?
I think of those believers whose imagery can dress them
sentimental bodies of Christ, all flogged and white,
the nail-holes slowly changing back, then gone
into hands and hearts of the saintly, or deluded.
Or Buddha's lotus body, or the Bodhidharma thousand armed:
I ache to think I carry those around!

I think of Monroe's fear of ageing
stopping so abruptly, as if the spirit was
a petticoat slipped off, leaving nothing.
The haunting image. I saw an old man at the shop
with dandruff and a face so lined it might have grown
through a string bag (his spirit in string, held in and down
and just too small?) Time can make the heavy body light,
or the light heavy, this difference quite extraordinary.
I go on looking. But as Rumi said centuries ago (stuff him!):
what you are looking for is what is looking.

For My Son

Is this how the spirit-body moves? First
as sky-days when the blue fell in upon you
(you would say now — as though karateed)
you grappling with this body recalling angels
and what a rough bloody lot they'd been
just getting you born! You are how it sees
daylight and the world of dreams.
Your father and mother watch over you
in a darkened room.

What association does it have? Those
misty ecstatic mornings when I carried you
to see Bully and Heif, the landlord's
young cattle, their black cross-bred heads
bunting me for the tickle that made *you* laugh!
That, and the hieroglyphs I drew
along their damp and dewy bodies.
The sun crept up beside us, grazing on the mist.

What kind of speech? The times
when your mouth utters the unexpected thought
I am about to speak, or ingenious excuses
if my mercurial anger shifts onto your skin.
The time I came back from the mailbox with you
a twelve-month-old speaking perfectly by signs.

When you are paralysed with laughter
when we stop playing parents, all three joining
the great plait of characters from books
each with a place but each so intimate.

How does it grow? This spirit of child?
You are nearly six years old
(is the timeless in such a rush to age?)
muscles hard as cricket bats.
Abruptly you will be the next size up.
The world gets more and more grip on you.

Spirit to the Body

When I've kissed you, made love with you
I've kissed the flat surface of the Estuary
where the air is glassy but the sand
shimmers like a warming body. I've tasted
the sun and turned over on its belly,
I've felt the long intimate throat of the sky.
Such is the after-taste. And so I make
the world in the prospensity of love, being
sensuous, lusty, and generous.
And sometimes cold. On sharp nights
I lie down among the sheets of frost
each of us miniscule and white.

I curl up into the Olgas, where the endless
being of the world has worn us down
into these woman-rocks, or the man-bunched
shoulders, the bent knees, outrageous testicles
and I am naked, walked upon by stars,
fed from the intricate surfaces:
crystal, insect, leaf, each at a time
fed into the air, levering upon the sun
to feel each day roll over me.

I wait, imbedded in a southern cliff,
the weight of land behind me, like a great spine,
the wind in my ribs of limestone.
I am the washed and wind-altered
skeleton, harbour of birds from their pushing
ocean-world of air below the constant
moving walls of consciousness, this other ocean
moving in, fold upon fold of the cerebrum.

There is no language but the sensory here,
where the whole universe longs for body
and ululates from all things solid. Even
the sky is a plank balanced upon my hip, its breath
fills into the red bewildering vowels of country
the staggering round-wind and rain rocks
the shatter-block consonants of ranges, iron-breeze.
Here are genitals laid down in stone and river,
the pubic matting, the gum-laden aromatic trees.

This is the dance we make together
having come to terms, finally.
I enter the solid, you divide down
like a tree narrowing constantly from the trunk
until each sliver of twig or bud breathes
vapours that are teeming worlds, down to
where my power-world populates your atoms.

The Poet as Columbus

for Bill Hart-Smith

That addled block of flats in King George St,
hammers of the work-site, our conversations.
Above us, tenants argued drunkenly, their voices
like the shriek of pulleys. And the constant
tongues of radios: DJs in those years
parroting Americans. We leant over the rail,
above the dull-coloured shallows of the carpark
and spoke of mysteries, the two of us
touched by the intuitions of the sufis,
or the crank-like machinations of Gurdjieff.

Now we have two times, two cities.
Perth, Auckland. At first we were good:
another letter, another cassette, your eyes tired, my talk
intermittent; I raved on through traffic sounds
as I drove to work. You could hear each thought
surge like a gear engaged. And yours came back
among the clicks and stops of the microphone
as though a Bushman sat beside you.
But a little sense escaped us!

I thought so strongly of Columbus
as all those years before, you wrote of him . . .
on days skimming westward and returning, carrying
the sphere with him. His eye, at least,
satisfied: matter and spirit were
the swirling lines around a body.

We write and speak no more, but now I hear
illness breaks on you again, old friend.
You travelled there before, and returned:
two voyages of death healing in your brain.
You emerged to days, amazed that journeying
so ravaged the hull; that the wood-worm of haemorrhage
would persist. But all this as a younger man
who did not find the mists there permanent
as now you must, unworldly, going blind.
You must take the sphere with you
where inside spin memory's and the moment's mad electrons,
swirling lines around a body.
Eastward, westward.

Perhaps Columbus rises through the floor
confronting you, with chest and chains
in a dark room. But the metaphors should link
and gleam of living: you live and will die
not a sufi or a mariner, but a poet.
Your chest is ours as well, is packed with poems.
Who knows if the latest accolades
catch the light and gleam inside your darkness,
they are no less solid. They remind
those of us who never needed it and those who did,
for all this bitterness of illness
your works persist, tough and whimsical and pure.
Nothing more or less than a life.

So long since we have spoken. Illness too, did this.
When I think of your life, your poems, I think
of you collecting cowries at the sea's edge:
their eyes filled a quarter-wall of boxes in your room
and seemed, in time you said, like a stranger's.
See them now in their tubes,
eyes squinting through the glass.
You stare at them, they stare back.
Something is being answered.

Cityprints

I dream in fibreglass. (I am fantasy, launched in the mind
like quarks, full of charge and theory, but no mass.)
I am the one Paul Newman eye that stays unblinked: the pool
with its long-handled lids and its make-up and its fluttering
    motors.
I am the extra room, the compact discs set spinning to
    toughen out my
restlessness, the high consoling sound of the second car, the
    appliances
placed like sculptures inside rooms. These are my acts of
living.

*   *   *

My stutter-birds arrive for summer, favour lawns
for their glassy droppings, leap and fan-jump,
tail-swinging, worrying or clacking, swishing their subtle
    plumage,
their dreamy spectrums. These are my tiny angels. To redeem
the sands and mores, the lived-on, levelling sands and
    assumptions,
the artifacts of applause. I absent myself, wakeful in the heat
saying: grow me, give me body! I am the tile-thick reptilian
    roofs,
the flair and evolution, faster than I know, of going
    somewhere . . .

*   *   *

My lines leave deep, elaborate gestures, done in a kind of
    illness
beneath the eyes, across the cheeks, foreheads. Here is the
    head-line
cutting deepest, the head not the heart-line that is tempted,
    the head
knowing these curved streets and cul-de-sacs might if flung
    outwards
open like a ladder leading up, open like a fate-line leading out.
Only my millionaires stay young. They are my happiest
    apprentices.

*   *   *

I am TV waves, the viewing dollars: the sweep and whorls of
    isobars
where the great print is laid down, imperfectly, like all
    designs
upon us. I am electronic wheat dumped on your spiritless
    markets
by the riders of the combines. You buck and twist but soon
    enough
my languages are constant rodeo, are of falling and getting up
    again,
language teaching the user, language as vast and patient as
    weather,
or as this ocean flanked by languages. I teach you for the
    world.
I sing in your voices as I sing in anyone's; your labours keep
    the city
rational and almost honest; your pretences make no damage,
    lodge there
like the third act of Hamlet, giving out the truths you will die
    of.

*   *   *

I have thinned out by the airport. My grooves are cut
neat as a record: here I am a poor man's compact disc.
When the old laser of the sun plays me round
at dawn, rocks me awake, blues my limbs with overalls,
I turn out into tracks and trucks and fork lifts, my groin
     nudges
and lifts, my womb loves plastics, or hunkers in cavernous
     shifts.

*   *   *

My blood is everywhere red, leaded or unleaded; I flow
in a quandry of plastic tubes, I swing and spit and am never
in fashion. I wear the rough and thunderous clothing of jets
but never travel. Most of me is simple, doesn't give a stuff.
I see the sun setting over the city: officious beetle
rolling each workday between its legs − like a ball of dung.

*   *   *

Or is there nothing worse than knowing
that the lines join up, pull thin and thinner,
like web or radar sweeping one onto the other, until each of
     us
lies there when the lines have packed so close
they cut? Listen to the common music, of life.
Only when it is so sharp, is the singing
high and free, and then, perhaps, we fall
through the other side of language, through
the assertion of arteries, the nervousness of veins,
to where there are   no cuts, no surfaces, no lines.

Belonging

This is not the place
the last diesel pulsing across the darkness
this shape the end-of-night   its wheels spinning.

Forty garish frames of glass
where none are flattered
carriage glare equally disfiguring to all.
One voice flares like a lighter struck obsessively
but low on gas.   A young girl
rolls her tips   of Boy George hair
light hits   the stoic pensioners
hits   my hands whitely on my lap.

We do not pretend to see. This is not the place.
As the line cuts the city open like an operation
and we stare at vague or vital organs.

This is not the place
to ponder what happens next as doors gasp and release
three into the night, the platform cold and bare.

This is not the place
the driver invisible as power, the speech of steel.
Between the curvature of glass this ampoule of city
where light is hitting out,
and seeing is retinal, shimmers like a scar.

This is not the place.
The billboards loom
and depart   Alpine or army ads, slick, insensible,
everywhere expensive, unanswerable.
This bright illusion as we stare.

The Chamber and Chamberlain

The courtroom is underwater opera, aquarium for the deaf.
Counsel and judge flit and pause, mouthing like goldfish,
nuzzling down onto flakes of law, minutiae on the pages
grown like coral. Lines of bubbles stream from the jury —
justice utterly bewilders them, as it should. To compensate,
truth leans twelve different ways, attempts the muscle
of concentration, but who is sure if the jury are swimmers
or singers or part of the set. Justice is the biggest
bubble of the lot. The mumbled points of conceptuality
never prick it: here are the sharks grazing against
the glass. Only the judge remains exotic, his scales
strobing porphyrian above proceedings, or flashing
from the mirth that no-one else is quite permitted,
putting personality where it isn't. The accused stares
with desperate equanimity. She's an example they won't take.

Inside the Cultural Centre

I view the hanging Bacons. The Pope's
robe is red as a toreador's cape
or the bull's streaming back. And faces
cut to violent rashes of red and white.
In rooms that slide off from the true,
bodies slump as if ropes have been removed,
gravity draws them through into the grey.

Here is the body like a corpse at sea,
insight beating on it like the waves,
crest and trough the one ironic unit.
I think of poets who put a voice to this,
Ted Hughes reading his poems of Crow:
that grisly carrion stalking
where old brains seize the new like the old
onto the new Testaments. Plath and Berryman,
who brought themselves up from that glare,
wearing poems like psychic flesh,
giving and going down.

Or dissidents, each word sung
from laceration; tortured once for speech
then once again, to keep them silent.
The people queueing each day for food
write the country's truest sentence.

Looking at Bacon, his enthroned Pope grimacing . . .
The red ghost has white teeth after all, shapeless

and beguiling. Purgatory is trying to reach through.
This art is a kind of vertigo we suffer from
staring down into the desperate room.
Do we approach too far, or does the heart recede?

Behind me the Gallery staff stand in uniform,
detached, indifferent. They never wrestle
the raw works back onto the wall — yet bodies
leap from it by the second.

A Demonstration of the Van der Graaf Generator for Children

The man in the Faraday rage is monkeying about
with electricity — it arc-welds light to this face,
it flirts with his assistant, whispering sweet nothings
through its blue flash spidery fingers, stands
her up hair first: brunette fashion spits Medusa,
writhes to hear the laughter from the children.
The show's a hit, care of Van der Graaf,
whose phallic generator whines and blasts
all the way from upper turrets of the castle,
where the Doctor cries out from his celebration
(now the assistant's part of his mythtake)
"By George! I think she's Gothic!"
It's as sexual as you make it.
Electricity leaps out, unseen through her fingers
if she holds the towering steel, the burnished glans,
it blasts the air in climax one and two
and when she stands back at last
it spurts into a can like a sample at the clinic.
Now the beast has finished, they close the gate,
the kids go loose and disappear with parents.
The demonstration's over, the earth has moved.

Glass 1: Creation of the Mirror

A glow spreads on the glass   but has no focus
then slowly one man's face   the polisher moves above you
his breath is mist   is this your face?

The polisher has left you wrapped   but the paper is a
temporary darkness   a kind of uterus you will emerge from
dreaming of   unwrapped by light.

You wait   an oval, bastard shape: no one formula
defines you   in turn you offer none   each face will be
the first   the equal   the perfect contemplation.

The carpenter   lifts you to the table   swirling wood-dust
modules of light   cling to the paper   his blue shirt
it's a fish   he laughs   a great flat fish.

Sssshhhh Ah   he tears you into light
flooding from the side-wall   the swung window divided into
     four
your first clarity   his face   you feed on light.

You slide into the wood   into this body   you are the clearest
coldest part   flashed across   stared into for minutes
motionless   pitiless   mute.

Glass 2: We Could Not

For days one of us carried it
wide and cold, like a weapon.
Then, at times, a frame
that spread beside us:
images filled behind it
like a sudden civilisation.
Nothing it drew in
sprawled or was slovenly.
We gasped the clear spaces
between trees, immensities
caught frost-angular.
At first it seemed the glass
was momentary. We were birds
flitting into the glass-like
images of flight, we fed
upon the clear-winged insects.
But we preyed upon ourselves,
were swallowed by reflections.
We forgot who found the glass,
forgot who held our way back.
When we looked into the glass
its objects were not before
but there behind us. We spoke
of equals, opposites, reversals,
we spoke of logic and of nonsense.
We saw each man and woman
build their lesser mirrors
from the silica of tiny acts.
Here was our new country, the new
being the old where the future
spreads like a clear immensity,
images flashing from frozen silk.
No one mind made a landscape,
it was created there by overlaps.
The sun did not swoop down

and take us up among its haloes.
Little among mere happiness
or there among the angry sheets
(for all their mirror-like faces)
came visionary or ecstatic.
Some wanted none of this
and so were satisfied to live
seeing nothing but their faces.
We could not carry ourselves
within ourselves wild and cold
as a weapon. We said a weapon
must have a target. We could not
duel with the image of a duel.

Varia

They are fronts, all further meetings
press like two flat sheets of glass together.
They grip in a fury of flat wrestling:
the more they push, the more impossible to part.

Slid into the light of any subject
they are uncannily alike; they squint into the mirror
they make each other, their mouthings
transparent, their logic in tiny lines that bite.

Perhaps . . . glass is horizontal in one
and vertical in one other, so light will polarise.
The picture clears, if you stand beyond them.
Or slip apart, as I have, being one of them.

Glass 3: Defection

They come for him before first light, but
he is lit regardless, by name and personal history,
by this dossier of flesh.

They come for him like linesmen, black angels
full of power — where identity is a fuse
that burns out in a blue flash.

Defection is the mirror by his bed. He leaps against it
presses his body into the glass, begins slowly
passing through it. He knows from the other side

he is caught between the mind's two countries
like a ballet star leaping between walls of mirrors.
At the point of panic, then past, the eye defects:

sees the snow-spread melancholy of the land, his cat
curled on her favourite chair, cutlery on the table's plain
    wood,
rows of foodstuffs, habitual, hermetic, the counter-argument

of cans along the shelf. He sees country in the two men
moving in, as they make a closing angle past the bed
the geometric curves and painted head.

They come for him but are caught up. The room
reeks of exile: a bin has split in the wretched kitchen,
the windows bare the chilling light. The cold floor, the bed.

Some part of them resists. It is worse than dream.
The man disappearing through the glass seems perfect.
Intensities ache upon their bodies but can't get in.

Their two-man status down to one and one, dark uniforms
alien at neck and wrist . . . They cannot take the mirror.
They stare at what is left of him: two still men.

The Fish

The fish was out-manoeuvred
to end here upon a block
most of the body gone, dissembled by a world
where the hyperactive is normal.
But it swims to me, reconstructed.
The carcase is aggressive, present,
its teeth the symbols of a vicious dreaming;
from the sockets of what is eaten,
the terrible occlusion of its eyes.

Even the intricate has force.
The startling gills of this fish
spike me into admiration
the esoteric manner of breath given over
to a simpler, larger form
where the oxygen is ants,
brown globules on busy legs,
where the mouth lets out
that cry into silence as death leaves
the red world of the throat.

Blue air has come, and even
the flesh turns against itself,
is transformed, is hungry, tenacious,
with molecules for jaws.
For days it seems endless,
the outbreath is doubly intense −
ants carry each piece off
like a crystal of sugar.
A crow comes, and the head
takes the air, lifts under black wings
like a bulky undercarriage,
like the pontoon of a sea-plane.

TV: The News, Whoopie Goldberg, Then the Invasion of Hungary in '56

1

Starting at the end this is what they give us:
Hungary. As the old black and white footage
freezes one circle I feel the tremor of containment,
as the small white circle drops like a halo
around a head: history laps the gaunt face.

A young man of the movement, standing on
a truck . . . the viewer is concentrated where
the cameras endow him, canonise him.
This saint of the people, this TV saint
as he became, sacrificed a day later.
That is, died well . . . he is the voice we hear
but has no sound-track, the tremor
on the other side of circles, meaning death.

I see another circle, but hear its voice
speaking clearly of the ranks, of the Soviets
he may, for all we know, outlive.
In colour now, he tells and tenses
with emotion the heady days they won
against the tanks, against the Arvo,
a man so English and Manchestered in accent,
he calls machine guns Tommys.
Just kids, heroic teens, and a woman
who took lead in her lungs, as now her circle
speaks the US accent where she lives.
These two have spoken well, and nerves
inside their circles tell me how that dream
has left them the tremor of the living.

What moves me always: the coldly wrong
oppression is, like an evolutionary thumb
that works against the fingers, not to hold
but to fumble grip and decency.

The name of brutality, if name explains,
slips the tongue, is like a new concept
in physics: a force or reaction made once
makes each repetition easier.
It's thinner than air, and steps aside
after the bullets strike, slips just like
life slips its tiny heaven from the body.

I weep not for the suffering alone,
but for this absence, this cold condition:
the imagery of which comes down to us
like photos on a plate, like the meaning
from a line of words. Orphan:
having morphology not parentage.

2

This is what they give, this is giving.
Before the programs, the news: here the tremor is
two readers, grinning arpeggios in unison,
figures turned on and off by ratings.
This man-and-wife-impersonation, and bizarrely
this is what they give us, this is giving:

a body on the street in South America
like a dropped wine-sack lying in red.
The Princess, Mills and Booness, dressed in sugar.
Shovels on strike, policemen on the take.
Whales nuzzling at ice like big, thinking
bubbas, workers talking in clouds, aiming for the sea.

All this is what they give us,
rendered equal, between advertisements
for Hondas, quick-cuts, pools, bank interest;
food and death, served up like a kilo of brisket.
Nouveau kitsch, before the news readers
again show up, proud as perfect parents.

On to Whoopie Goldberg. Hollywood
goes over the top in light machines.
This what they give us, of the species,
imagery that blocks the room like floss
that clears only when a channel-change gives Hungary.
Bullets and the universal stink of diesel engines
wipe away the gaudy serials, wipe in irony
because this story comes directly from
the house of humanity. For all its absence and its
wrong condition, it has our tremor, our condition.

Visit to the Omni Theatre

Not fully three-dimensional but wrap-around
— like sitting in the blunt end of an egg —
the screen is white before the film has run
but once it's on it wants to be another world
and suddenly is: perspective cracks and drops,
my stomach slips like raw egg on a plate.

A film shot from helicopter:
rotors cut against the upper screen
like hand-spun reel mowers. The bluish
air keeps falling down forever
blue as harbour, blue that lives in dream
falling past the beating edge of cortex
with grunts, or crazy laughter: *ha ha ha ha ha ha*

like being in another country, all eyes and wordless,
the rise and fall of making love, again and again.

The camera's swung, but now it's us,
half dopey like astronauts, oddly naked to off-gravity,
as if to that Scots scientist who may yet make us weightless
with gyroscopes. We're unaligned, like the two
half and brilliant mirrors in theodolites.

The frames of film go past but even as I laugh
my son admits he's lost, what he sees is like
the colour that has missed the face in comics.
If it was not about old planes, maybe something R,
the film gives going down a different meaning:
the screen wrapped round like legs, and I'm the mouth
— or, perhaps, the opposite. World is inside us, not out.

Something thrills the scenes together and apart
like images on a pack of cards the grinning cardsharp
spreads and shuffles with his deft applause.
So we stare at something fixed, a chair,
or the lower edge, or the person's head in front,
to slip the vertigo of dreaming, or laughing, or making love.

Children at Climbing Games

Watching them is to watch the past, images
I hope won't come again — of falling
emptily from trees, finding wire like a pull-through
in my finger, or crashing bikes down
onto concrete, my knee as side car
tearing into a spray of red sparks
that kept on when I'd stopped.
I caught the graze and power of it
but not huge breakage, never loss.
Now superstition gambles me, to think
luck will not fall down in the same place twice
(or maybe does, landing like two-up).

Such virgins of the surgery as myself
make the worst witnesses. Because
I have held him at night, or smiled
arm in arm, inches from his face,
I know the strange flesh a child is,
soft as only prayers can be,
or meditations, things non-physical to me,
but powered etherally as the sufis say,
into a form so subtly awesome,
regardless of shape or size or personality,
the crooked, the slow, the lame,
given and received through the gods
we cannot touch, or see. Watching them
is to watch those crises of the past,
like jowling down beside the dog to see
if this time the bugger will bite,
changed crucially: someone soft is doing them.
Because the prayer has flesh
and blood. And rides on bikes,
and climbs up trees.

Jussi Björling

The great Swedish tenor, who specialised in Italian and French
Opera. Considered by many to be one of the greatest tenors ever,
he succumbed to alcoholism towards the end of his career.

1

Drunkenness is slowing down the targets —
the room, yourself —
off-night catharsis. Mind and body go manic
whack the big notes like karate

but the hotel-room set
only lasts the first performance:
that bull-like tenor's body
making matchwood of tables, chairs.

You've got the score by memory.
It becomes the record that repeats itself.
Others raved at parties, intent on legend.

You fought alone, another monstrous stylus
creeping in: the brooding
verismo of despair.

I think of the hugest opera singers — the whales,
their bodies drummed upon by music
their opera to stir and humour in dark waves.

There too each brain has the score by memory
and it seems that aria is decompression
(that heady lift of "Nessun Dorma" in your famed recording).

But then as if the depths were alien and cold
they can lose their places
their appalling bodies on the beaches.

2

There's a scratch on the disc of history
the needle catches and can't move past: the catch-lines

of the great thin-lipped one: *Caruso sings a high C*
like a cavalier throwing down a gold sovereign. He doesn't.
    The aria's

transposed down to save this greatest "baritone" from
    shrieking!
How *beautifully* his legend sings, *how majestically,*
    incomparably, how

like a God (who bellows, shows-off, sobs!). But threw out
    everything,
sang into the fault-line of mastery and sheer abandon.

Caruso paced the street in spats, twirling a cane, his collars
    lined
with mink. When Bjorling paced, it was to scan the doorways

vulnerable to sound: from the bars came a blast like sirens,
whisky on the rocks

                    a Nordic Oldysseus
bloodless with stage-fright, delaying his reappearance;

victim to shot after shot of panicky indifference
two-handed whiskeys in the downtown pysche

on line to the '50s, the Zeitgeist of poets consumed
by voice, and anti-voice (its bloody pound of flesh).

There's no worse master. Think of Ibsen, Bergman, their
    chthonic power;
and there is Bjorling's head-power, his tense ambivalent heart

like the intensifying duel of Lensky, arias after alcohol
Bjorling drunk on stage the double-basses grinding inexorably.

3

To know all this was to see you
open-mouthed between mirrors
fearing you would disappear at the infinite
fault-line. But you haven't.

Days before your death, that last expansive
Lohengrin, the Rangstrom song, Sibelius' intense
Black Roses. The brilliant gold of Bjorling sound.

Singing after heart attacks (Merrill saw your heart
almost punching holes in your costume) with each
outpouring a risk, who cares about disaffected stagecraft;
(besides – now there are only records).

The brass scoops and explodes, cymbals scattering
the harsh, too brilliant sunlight, the heart
that pounds there beside its silent twin, recording
all that has been and is still to come:

the slow, monumental build up, the massive lift,
modulations that astonish, as if the voice could
step-up evolution mid-phrase

as the diaphragm pumps the voice white-hot
the back-shivering power,
the seismic B flats . . .

                    and you open-mouthed
the man standing there, utterly, about to sing.

After Dinner Music

The table cleared
I flatten my palms on the wood
hearing the cello and bassoon
jogging Mozart.

Across the night
cicadas set up something by Grappelli
sweet and pizzicato on violin
and their others

are percussionists
in way-out skins, syncopating bodies
racketting their tymbals, spacing out
their double drumming

fast as nerves.
Until the radio's quarter century of valves
goes fractious: shrieks and bangs
then settles down.

I think of Ludwig
his tempers, his jagged late music
and lightning that hours ago twitched the wires
above my head

attacking this
old radio: electric spits and splutterings that flaw
the music, intrusions from a storm-world
less than Mozart.

Wolfgang the perfect.
He never was, but received the thing complete
taking down his compositions like an aerial
in harmonic winds.

In Beethoven the storm
rages and abates but I'm drenched and shaken,
I trip in ditches, crashing headlong
into isobars

that catch emotion.
Their lightning glares upon the staves of heaven.
But now the storm has gone. The water-pump makes constant
evening's heartbeat.

Magpies in trees
are drinking and spilling silver, fugues the cicadas
cannot resist in joining. I hear mosquitoes bowing
on the highest string.

Morso

1

Heat is tapping its hard and fugal fingers
down the red enamel of the wood-stove.

Entropy. All things lose heat. Entropy.
I say it to myself knowing sometimes

it happens in the night that all
my precious statements come to nothing.

I think of old composers (now quite dead)
whose every note is treated with respect.

Fingers at the keyboard make no judgment,
pianos shiny as enamel cannot hear

if the music's like a B flat bag of statements
that some inclement mind thought up at night.

And not for once the wood-stove taps
as heat and word enamelling wear thin.

We live among the scrutiny of the cold. Only
the sun and God see equally. Maybe more so.

2

The heat of putting one word with another.
Now it's chosen. What other source will do?

But music's too vigorous comparision — remember
Beethoven's hard fingers left keyboards wrecked:

grooves worn down into the ivories
like time warps, blurred and digital recordings

for the deaf. First himself, then the rest.

3

I hear the stars tapping at night where sky
is a fixed idea, vacuous and everywhere.

Words are naked, more wearing, more elusive
not spread out like a keyboard or a sky.

Words like jokes — give and take at the same moments,
sometimes they give and carry off the heat.

I think of warmth, from writers who've come before me
— their mettle's there, the heat, the tapping out of signs

— and worry if I'm good enough to follow.
Creation should be more than just a habit.

The night grows canny with its promises. The tune
ended, I'm hot, or cold, as the woodstove. Maybe more so.

This Far from the City

This old man across the road
wakes his ninety years and bellows for the ozone.
His skin is evidence: shot through by tiny suns
and left shockingly with living scars.
The rage will settle. He'll put the Communists
to rest for now, stagger out as always
on two sticks, two times a day
shuffling down his gravel furrow.
In winter it's a certain sign of rain.

Last year he nearly died, banged at my door
with the pad he wanted me to sign
below his anxious scrawl: his will.
He looked fit to kick the commies year by year,
wear down the queue before his cataracts were due.
It's just the heat, I said, *the heat.*
I won't sleep, he said, *won't sleep*
in case I never wake. Never mind the weather,
sign my will.

        Never mind unending things,
as now he seems. Stumping down his track
seeing each stone in or out of place,
foot after foot, as the world
turns beneath him, like a child walks a drum.

Never mind the weather, but under
that one universal constant
all week I am burning, worry at conservatives
or drink the slow hours into lethargy
or paddle at the blackness with a fine-point.
What small corruptions is he caught at
this close to the path where he hangs on.
Or that week he wouldn't sleep

for fear of dying? There is nothing I can say.
The vegetation murmurs, breathes in
among the suburbs. In talk he smells
the bong-end of big or little drug hauls;
the smell of lubricated rubber; the power
of modern women, the powerful smell of change,
the government's cover-up on ozone
ultra-violet searing in and order
from the old world's bottle, leaking up like rain.

Gaunt, garrulous, less than well,
his world goes spinning off the record.
Until he shuffles, two times a day, DJ at talkback,
or weatherman, with needle or stick, playing answers,
risking rain, deepening his barometric furrows.

The Kiss

Just so sensually
erupt from bunkers
these lethal lipsticks
Lucretia Borgia kisses
but these are male
and are made over distance.

Any lipprint that remains
will not patronise a new
renaissance, the pout
will close and the wild
woman will also slump
into the poison. The half-
death on her lips is now
half-life in the potion
but this is only irony, for
it kills everything. It's male:
less volatile, more thorough.
The white long-bearded
man in the sky, is yet
a prolific grower from spore
his body the feared mushroom
the champignon of brain-stem
and for so long in the dark
those small deceptive roots
will drag out everything.
The kiss sits on him
like a frog on a toadstool.

Properties of the Poet

Fingers and joints for all kinds of tension, also the muscles
of the neck. You've seen these held back until the throat
is like a sleeve packed with wire – they poke into the
     head-nerve . . .

Shoulders for dejection, joining the above; and joining
     downwards
to the stomach, this master cylinder of anxieties, which is
     vaulted
back to the upper chest for ecstasies (everything is so close).

Be leg-long for the various gaits, for leverage on bodies;
the legs – which balance chest or breasts and take you up
     against . . .
and are wishbone for leading upwards into . . . the apex.

Thigh-skin, the blind-skin of lips and throat for explorations,
the place of the apex itself – the begetting and beguiling
     sex-parts
for sex, for dreams, for dominations, for balance and
     abandon.

Thumbs of course for gripping, this human
hand-fang and its double, ghosting in the brain
like a hologram. Sometimes for letting go again.

General skin and skin to wear the touch-prints of things
     unseen.
Neck-hair, and the small metaphors of the goose
for fear, sudden knowledge, for the hot and chill emotions.

Red and deep voltages and laughter and a heart to shake
(you convulse therefore you am) from anger, loving, irony,
others from the above, from the darkly depressions.

The bottom of the feet — for instincts, the sudden kind
that speak in sweat, and perhaps long-drawn for
    apprehensions,
for the slow mastery of plodding through the world.

A head for speech, wires for connections and therefore
sometimes for pain, a head for time shifts for the knowing
    abyss
that sense-storms populate, colloids in the tea-brew of
    abstractions.

Finally, to the modern surfaces and the primal undercurrents
of the eyes and ears, essential colour jinkers and tone pullers;
these power-holds on attention, and sometimes pretend
    thinkers.

There's more, but these will do. These and the way they must
    be held
to know the times, to question the times into intensity.
And maybe come off even. It's not the sort of thing you win.

Passing Flats I Once Lived In

My flat-mate was my name-sake
but my opposite. I was brash, argumentative,
he turned his hands up, calm as cliche.
Pages rose in me, sharp, mad, ambitious,
his light tunes lingered on piano, content
as envelopes. He rose early, I
worked late. We hardly met. It seemed
two Philips made a psychiatric term
for diametric difference. It would
be right, like Heisenberg, to ask
which one of us would be there
when the lid was lifted? Because
since then I've often noticed
how my one opinion turns into its opposite.
One day I'm all against police,
next I fill the streets with law and absence.
I feel grief and hatred for the barbarous
but shudder at the blank there that is innocence.
Something about this is a line
not wanting to repeat itself,
where moving on is urgent, and seems
to promise revelation. Unlike the Philip
who played on among the ripples of himself,
like the minor variations up and down
the scale he played once for me
on harmonium, always turning back to theme.
Decisions such as these are touched
from preference, like chords, in certain keys,
but mine seem snatched, staccato,
make a modal or then a modern music
that half the time I won't believe in,
even for the biggest themes: for days,
within my chest, I am convinced of God
as simply as cool water on a summer's day
seems right. Or sudden silence, or laughter

when making love, seems right.
Yet I hear the line unplay itself
when the world touches me so badly, or so well
I stay fiercely, profanely human,
which seems right, like the candle I once burnt
down into its glass container, down
among the chords of slow depressive music
cracking the glass just as the pity died,
seemed right. If now I laugh at this
in that crack is silence, in the vagueness
is silence, in my changing passions
is silence, in the hesitation is silence.
In silence, is the terrible and worldess truth
telling me to lay down certainty upon the table
like a decapitated head, and watch it
jabber on regardless, all lips and teeth.
Returning to it later, I'll find the head
tranquil, eyes open, dignified.
The flat I passed, I once lived in.
The tragic/comic masks upon the wall
have gone, the keyboard this alter-ego
played upon has gone, the candle's
glass container has gone. Something
like the line not wanting to repeat itself
started there, a natural if disagreeable
contrariness. And as simply as cool water
on a summer day, it seems right.

Thinking of Rendra

As Mahomet said, talking of location —
Spirit (and I rephrase, for writers — Language)
lives closer in you than your jugular.

In that country so attuned to music
there are intervals so sensitive to spirit
the keys play silent. Jail for counterpoint.

Years before, writers had by order to juggle
a central, bastard language, because their own
was taken from them. Silence for counterpoint.

To juggle with a central or bastard conscience,
to speak at all, was knowing the sensual and the fierce
throat of utterance, locked from counterpoint.

The state is central as the lamp in shadowy wayang,
where characters are more than silhouettes, ancient
as status quo. Where one voice is many voices.

The *saron's* tongues are pinched by fingers, thumbs,
and *bonangs* stand in their brassiness like a row
of breasts, or soon more truly like a row of heads.

As the players at the centre strike down so exactly
the padded hammers, so certain they can tell
where the gongs finish and the heads begin.

The wayang plays, the gamelan plays, counterpoint
holds, and the shunned voices rattle in the night,
spin and burn like glow-worms in the throat.

saron: tuned metal bars suspended on a frame
bonang: tuned gongs, in rows, which play the main tune

A Migrant Woman Makes Her Choice

They must work within
the long male dream of factories and shop-floors:
women to work the moving steel, or the boning blade
this eye gone thin and sharp, slivering against the bone,
the left hand in chain-mail; St Joans,
cursed to hear male voices, to labour for their compelling
    vision.

And here is the armour of overalls, and caps
to hold their dark hair back from the wheels
from the naive Adam-nakedness of machines:
cylinders sliding and entering, the damn damn
of steel stampers closing onto the block, all bed and screw
and dreams of oil. These love-symptoms of the new-world.

To be material: Mika in a backroom
young alabaster Poland, modelling what she makes by day.
These most sensual of skins — the silks, the boss's eyes, her
    survival's
overtime. She is taken for his single Tivoli, but he can no
    more take
than lift the gleam from a streaking steel bobbin.
He must fail upon the curve of her widow-neck.

His eyes speed her slightest movements: the green silk
spilling down her shoulders, the nudge against her bodice.
His eyes on her, or hers at his machine; the pain is universal
but not the choice — nations take foreign women for labour
not for sex . . . Here in the thrum of English she can turn
    ironic heel
on blindness, the stain on her forehead that is patriarchy.

Her body lifts into a sky, both white and dense,
intense black letters are the stars in constellations,

she is unaware that aural rhythms lift her hair.
Her action is made speculative language, is made the imagery
exploited here; she is the primal, sensual body
we gift ourselves. She is naked as these words.

At her bench, the air itself is fabric
sewn by the fast approving *hmm* of the machines
this metal language becoming as familiar
as neighbourly invective. Nineteen other women beside her;
nineteen pairs of hands flit against her skin
in making each silken gown, and its shame.

At times they wail with Europe, drunk
on their sherry-stories, sombre, sweet, and then so fractious
the taut cheeklines, the widening lips
baring the shameless arguments they will cry over, to find
        remorse
rather than a bitter exploitation. Hoping
for all the bastards in it, life is yet handmade.

When she parades, silk-eyed, dressed in her green wind,
she is twenty women, suffering and soft
beneath the machinery of men. Only their attentions
hide her flesh, only their common fingers bring her back
from words or from the blue and nervous country of his eyes
from where her foreign self waits to be undone.

Vandalising the Bronze of Yagan

Statues are alien to the Aboriginal
but never mind. This one pays off a debt knocked up
by those other chisellers — the cultural hit-men.
This one fights their black scrabbled statues,
deadly ones of ink and letters built on white:
Aborigines in a wild grotesquerie of cowards
killing only from the back, and then only
killing in the soft-lands — of women, children.

Yagan is here, warrior and recognised as one,
even if bronze is a white cliche for black.
The water pipes the vandals coiled
like a metal python at his throat
and rammed between his legs,
have not in the slightest broken him:
they make the sculpture come alive.
Yagan, dead as metal, packs a fight.

I can almost hear water
singing in the pipes; hear a drone
starting in the player's lungs, end
in bird-shriek, hear the love of wrong relations
end in retribution. Pipes
bend under this land, singing;
no vandal can touch them,
they rise into this bronze, of Yagan.

The Commonwealth Poetry Readings

During the Tour of Britain, 1987

We stand and turn creation over
page by page. We came from warming continents,
from the long and chilling tramp through rain.

Now the walls want nothing of speed
and their face-sapping closeness
worry the words from us, a panic of acoustics.

The audience must wonder why they strain.
As each of us perform, our skins and words
become the atlas anyone can hold.

Its general format is humanity.
If sometimes even this becomes oppressive
forget it — each reader's new inflection

lays a sensuous outline, each colour
nods and then escapes the frail entwining nets
of race, of latitude and longitude.

Forget one sound of this tongue we share
called English — each night we show a different city
five new versions of it, passionate, exact.

Days before, the parallel: the London tube.
The carriage filled with faces, white and black
set into a long and staring silence, caught among

the jumbled rhythms of the tracks, between acts . . .
Blurred nothingness, words shrugged down shirtfronts
or spilling dryly, like dandruff onto shoulders.

Caught among other nets, of routes and destinations,
carriages, slugging along the lines, I would speak
how Britain took much from its colonies, giving words;

but now has pulled them in, tight, like a poem
and taken the words back, made them local dialect,
not for art, humanity, but cooler, cold as labour.

We take a taxi back, as we should have come.
Silently, given commonality by common transport.
Go off to our rooms. For a night the world is over.

Guest-House

The door may be the best part
but I check this first: whether there is brass
to speed the wood, and the price with it,
whether the bell-touch is warm and lit
(I want the world at my fingertips
or perhaps there on the tip of my tongue.)
Once inside and making my request
of the man or woman who stands there like a second door
that I inspect. Even as they move
to one side on a hinge of promises
will pillowslips be as crisp as her blouse,
the windows as clear and the street below
as busy as her eyes? Is it her world or his?
The man's unshaven; have the sheets cooled
and the towels dried from someone's skin?
Upstairs I taste the room, balanced
squarely by these two selves upon the city
and say yes, it will do. More or less.
Each of its ghosts, each blotch on their skin,
each smile that says you are a stranger
— but then looking down from the window
seeing my wife and son still in the car
isolates me here, so I turn back
into the room with its sure illusions
no one else has lived here quite like us.
The ghosts are local and for their own reasons
said *yes, it will do.* More or less.

Radio Telescopes

We are visited by intuition
like a brilliant cat

suddenly appearing; in a darkened room
leaping down upon our shoulders.

A thousand, who knows how many, a million
upturned dishes in our brains . . . wait

as she drinks their silent milk.
Like the stars, it is not an aquired taste.

In the darkness there are no words, nothing.
Just the intermittent ambiguous purring.

The Welder Variations

Dollar suns spatter on the limbs.

There is hand and rod, and multinationals behind the black-
      smoked rectangle of glass;
those eyes, startling and blue at the seeing panel. The future
      sizzles, being born.

It dances there continuously: the rod is brought to heat, melts
      whitely into the choreography of metal.
Each dancer is naked, sensual inside the flux. In the beginning
      was the steel.

You stare down upon their fingers, hearing the intensifying
      crackle, the metal hissing
to see it is good, to see what swirls from the epicentre of your
      rods, your lightning-centred deals!

*   *   *

The structures bunch there, brilliant, intricate. The roadways'
      dark and hammered metal
lies flat upon the ancient body, winking beads zipped up its
      endless middle.
Buildings rise rhetorically, or hunker darkly in their steel
      like geometric animals,
eager for the operation (cranes reach down, great and constant
      tools) to be slim and rational.
Some find an alloy suit, go trendy in tinted shades or rise
      and race, sinuous and replete.
Some are wall-less, each floor poised: an iron crab up on thin

legs, but over-cooked by vertical thinkers;
or concertinas drawn up and out for air, their moaning like
    the sound of winds from the north-west:
the iron range a fallen source, pulled out and down . . . the
    long gasp lasting forever . . .

*   *   *

Rolling a cigarette. You're 19 or 50, male or female, come
    from Europe, Asia, born here as virtuoso.
In Europe it was cold that buckled metal, here it is the
    sky-rod burning for profit.
The country is a steel sheet; it is red exploited metal, tin-hat
    hills, hard-hat logic;
or closer in, the fenced off paddocks sigh as steel rollers gnurl
    their surface after rains;
disc and combine — wait for the murmuring colours of the
    inner heat-shift, the flames and corrosion
of phosphate, the seeds which turn the coppery surfaces
    green.

There are rivers that wind like heat-blued metal shavings
    down to the power-bench of the city;
the pace is hottest where the sun burns upon the water its
    pure acetylene. It dreams of oil.
Reaching the buildings the city is less the wound-up clamp
    upon it, than lips moving on the embouchure:
the future's modern and erotic music is hot, hotter, blows us
    out.

Barbecue of the Primitives

They stand in a roughish circle: a row of backs,
a muddling Stonehenge, half tourist,
half ritual. As the fire is carried out
in boxes, a male and dormant thing, assembled
from clinking cylinders, thin pipes
curling like snakes into the coupling place,
hissing until the match bomps them into flame.
The hot air pouts and silkens,
or crimps like someone beaming down in Star Trek.
The red portable ovens, standing
like UFOs and calling the wilderness
to sit around with its own ether blue as flame.

It pre-empts the liquor, and perhaps the light,
both will fall on the picnickers
like something strong, pre-figuring.
If the city stands fifty dry kilometres
towards the coast, under the radiation
of what it means to be human: this ether of bush
hits them like the weightless falling
of neutrinos, passing through without sensation,
like silent speech. But

only teeth will beam them back
to being primal, and the fire-juice of steaks.
It is the only time they give up speech.
They eat, as far above the sky convulses
outward to the tufted body of an eagle
high on ozone and the lean entirety of hunger.

Like pets, the cars sit under trees
or curl into their gloss out in the heat.
The insects now seem utterly demented:
each beat a coin in air's strict metre.
Something is being counted off, by ones.

Symphony and Song on the Black Fringe

Black   Black   Black
Fringe: meaning the outer population. Yes, and edges,
not fanatical or eccentric but maybe visionary,
perhaps diffractions yielding darkness, brightness,
or where we interfered with light. Yes, marginal,
but not ornament, not a false colour.

What do they mean by the gathered iron?
Are these dwellings metaphors for a new Dreaming
when there are no cities,

                          when metal is all we leave
at the wrong end of the chain of our productions?

These rest in the long sight of the city towers:
heads humming and alive with water-songs,
steel-ribbed, immanent, watchers over black and white;
Kadaichi men in glass.

                          But feel against the mind-skin
this rustling to a knife-edge, the black angers
clutched inside that paralysed storm of sheets.
Wild lives kick in this metal

                          each day until it's totem:
people cleave from the banging atoms.
Women, black, metallic.
Men, their faces case-hardened.
Older people, weathered, silent metal.
And children, vivid as stainless steel.

Then you see
mutilated iron fingers, noses bent out of shape,
an eye hanging from the ruptured metal.
The damage knocks the women onto their backs
or down on all fours, a breast, a face
a brilliant gash where the hammer
glanced.

We came upon this shore like Vikings
cold gods from the North with dreams of Thor
wrestling the serpent off the Western Ocean.

Woke with the hammer in our hands,
where waking from another Dream is a memory
these people must forget

each day facing
the blinding rectangle of light
where the sheeted iron is open to the world.

The metal is hard, silent. It has these qualities.
Cut across, pieces removed (this causes
a tremor perhaps) does the injury say more intensely
what language doesn't?

They rise
buckled, bent, hobbling where a leg
is hammered short.

Who asks is there a spirit leg,
a dream of leg? Of the Dreamtime's post-generation,
the dispossessed: they have been dreamt by us.
Carried into the iron-age, first modern age of consent,
shaped by sudden blacksmiths:

Soldiers, pioneers with muskets, hammer-locks   *bang   bang*
The arm-lock of the Good White Sisters   *bang*
Children, from neck to neck the gossamer chains of religion
     bang
Arsenic and jaw-lock   *bang   bang*
Gave way to the first sociology: black velvet   *bang*
Gave way to the caste of too much white man's flour   *bang*
Gave way to alcohol and its generous pains   *bang   bang*
To four walls and a barred door   *bang*.

*   *   *

Ironies. A white poet
another garrulous white
                    wandering through images
of broken houses: a heap of floorboards on the gas stove
charcoaled, black, burnt-out in the centre.
Broken windows, walls, choked toilets,
blue paint flaking into sequins.

Ironies. Talking to white advisers
who acted without a thanking smile,
somehow, having smiled upon themselves.
Who pumped themselves for several years then collapsed.
Black holes? White dwarfs?

Or to shift the metaphor a little
perhaps no more than Tilley lamps
brilliant but then run out of fuel
below the frail white mantle.

Ironies. How to see through modern eyes
a people both carnal and religious,
gentle but violent, artists who have gone
down into the bottle like white men
but now begin to burn without it.

Who lived out the great myths
unconscious people doing *this* consciously.
Laws intricate as the packed red string of headbands
worn within the blood.

But then to sit around in turns bellicose or sad
scuffling to draw each other's
red, iron smell of blood. Or vengeful blood:
the woman who stabs the old white drunk in sex
and cuts the long pink strap between his legs
lives out two hundred years of bad blood.

It twists the nostrils
where old souls rear up re-newed.
None had said before of white initiations,
none had left their later souls at land's end
for the people to draw on, fully-clothed.

*   *   *

The people return to their place of Iron, to the place
of Unofficial Village, their 40° or freezing beside the metal.
But their voices disturb — the sceptics a dull white Rainbow
they must resist where once it swallowed them, vomiting rust.
They re-enter the river-city like those with land
have waited as the spirit waits, drunk with shape.

The fringe has mouth for love and argument and drink,
oral world, the spirit alive beneath the tongue.
For the Second Time the mouth does what the heart has
        known,
to create, to argue, to condemn: where white was Dreaming
and called it black:

                        at the place of Paternalism, the place
of Useless Men, the place of Unbelief, of Lost Land,
the place of Alcohol, the place of Fighting with Flagons,
        the place
of Easy Arrest, three great-places-in-a-row of
Paddy-Wagon   Court   Prison,
the places of Staying Drunk, of Happiness Just Now,
of Children's Smiles before the grief place, the ghost
place of Infant Mortality.
The place of No Easy Answers, of No Votes In Boongs.

But now the one and further place
of Future, suddenly loud, passionate,
the one both sides withheld.

Train Trip across the Nullarbor

What position do I travel in? Find a satisfactory angle
from the upright, go shimmy-hipped, or shilly-legged
let my feet make a mild announcement in the aisle.
How do I speak, why, and to whom, in this land of neutral?

I hardly see the man with the raddled skin one seat down
but snatch glances at the woman beside him − so alike
someone, yet not, so that her differences makes me check
      again and again
as my image returns, and then moves away from me like a
      station.

Children dense to custom and ignored by parents, wander too
searching for the mythical lost faces; they'll know when they
      see
these could be anyone's. Adults keep eyes averted, go
      flat-faced
and simple, having long ago learnt to blank out their features.

Outside, the continent is not travelled, it *departs*.
The plain has lost perspective; space is flat. It's either lit
by daylight or it's not. We sit as astronauts in a long straight
      squirt
of water, the spectrum on the inside and spinifex like dull
      asteroids.

The stops hit unexpectedly, have no nationality, no language.
Nothing happens before the train begins again, as if it too
forgets itself, and stops to meditate on the sheer tracks.
At sidings it rests one arm on the ten metres of platform.

We step awkwardly onto the planet, into spaces between us,
like strangers standing outside, then packed inside, a lift.
We need to talk, assert the sill of words upon the scene,
shift in the intra-space, the camouflage of couples or families,

caught as we are between significance and this sketch of
    street,
walls done in straightish lines the sun has pushed so far off
    true
that light seems more major here than gravity. If the stop was
    made
for the necessary renewal of our gravity, then it has failed.

When the train accelerates and shakes off this outer force
we realise the other G of train, its subtly kneading palms
moving us into the aisles; forwards, backwards, playing
    relativity;
arranging meetings; the semi-transport of our words,
    gestures . . .

the train keeps on . . . deep-muscle masseur, of the sober or
    drunk;
worker at the strong or wounded characters of our jokes and
    dreams.
Using age, sex, dress, as many signs as move us in the
    labyrinth
like a constant semiology, disguising us to give us life.

The punk with fierce hair and studded yellow jacket
reads a text on native flora and fauna (perhaps he's in it).
An old man in a suit, sleeps on the bar-seats one up from
    the girls.
A young couple giggle under their rug, have invented
    moveless sex.

I see a young man's hand-slip of pills, his miniature carriages,
as he slinks into the jagged room, leaves us flat and darkened,
for the broken skyline of his dreams. A hand draws down
from the reading light — a five-limbed light-fish sinks

into ocean . . . The seats are empty. My heart jolts like a
    shunted
carriage, and so the next carriage and the next.
The carriages are a long shuttling series of rooms.
They are my own . . . sad or beautiful, until the lilac rooms of
    dawn.

You and our son, your brow and cheeklines softened by sleep,
    his hand
draped on your neck, his gentle Wookie. The book is still in
    the rug
where you ceased and slept halfway through the narrative of
    Star Wars.
We descend through mist. It is the sky we have come from.

The gimlets have gone, their pale bark hanging open like
    blouses;
and now the varied gums, a valley plunging slowly into forest,
rivers rushing at the loafing rocks and spawning ghost-rocks
of foam. The old world is new, comes back to recognition.

Air falls invisibly upon us. We begin fussing at the nerve-
    pouch
of our cases. The sun suddenly hits, runs like a vivid porter
down the aisle. The city spreads before us, intricate with its
    objects
of the future. So bold and geometric, this anti-copy of the
    Nullarbor.

More UQP POETRY

Thomas Shapcott *Welcome!*
Dimitris Tsaloumas *The Observatory*
Evan Jones *Left at the Post*
Philip Mead *This River is in the South*
Gary Catalano *Slow Tennis*
Cornelis Vleeskens *The Day The River*
John Blight *Holiday Sea Sonnets*
John A. Scott *St Clair*
Andrew Taylor *Travelling*
Dimitris Tsaloumas *The Book of Epigrams*
Richard Kelly Tipping *Nearer By Far*
Lewis Packer *Serpentine Futures*
Silvana Gardner *The Devil in Nature*
Michael Sariban *A Formula for Glass*
Thomas Shapcott *Travel Dice*
Susan Afterman *Rain*
Thomas Shapcott *Shabbytown Calendar*
Dimitris Tsaloumas *Falcon Drinking*
Michael Dransfield *Collected Poems*
Gary Catalano *Fresh Linen*
Bruce Beaver *Charmed Lives*
John Tranter *Under Berlin*
John A. Scott *Singles*
Judith Rodriguez *New and Selected Poems*
Bobbi Sykes *Love Poems and Other Revolutionary Actions*
Andrew Taylor *Selected Poems*
Charles Buckmaster *Collected Poems*
Tom Shapcott *Selected Poems: 1956-1988*